ACTIVATE YOUR ABUNDANCE

THE KEYS TO MANIFESTATION

ACTIVATE YOUR ABUNDANCE

THE KEYS TO MANIFESTATION

LUBNA KHARUSI

Dira

DIVINE • INTUITIVE • RECEPTIVE • AWARENESS
WWW.DIRAINTERNATIONAL.COM

ACTIVATE YOUR ABUNDANCE
THE KEYS TO MANIFESTATION
Lubna Kharusi
Published by Dira Publishing Limited
85 Great Portland Street
London
W1W 7LT
United Kingdom

www.dirainternational.com

Cover design by Lubna Kharusi

ISBN 978-1-912409-40-2

Dira

www.dirainternational.com

CONTENTS

This book includes the transcripts of a Dira workshop.
In order to buy the recordings for this workshop,
scan the QR code below.

ACTIVATE YOUR ABUNDANCE WORKSHOP

1. INTRODUCTION

A. Welcome

What is channeling?

One could say that we have all been channeling all our lives, but we tend to ignore it, as we all have intuition, insight, and inspiration, which is Divine communication through us.

Intuition is a part of human capacity and experience, but we have conditioned ourselves to turn down that voice inside us that wants to be expressed, by choosing logic and societal conditioning to take precedence. At Dira, we teach simple techniques of how to use self-hypnosis to turn down the dominance of the conscious mind and mental chatter, so that the voice of intuition and inspiration is clear and can be accessed on demand. We refer to this as channeling.

With the Dira channeling method, the guidance that then flows through you is that of The Divine Source. The Divine is a term used to refer to the Ultimate Source of Everything. Some say "God", others perhaps "Universal Consciousness"; there are many such terms, and you may use the word that resonates best for you that refers to Ultimate Source Energy.

For an extended Q&A on channeling, please visit
www.dirainternational.com

THE KEYS TO MANIFESTATION

B. The Contents of this Book

This book contains transcripts of channeled sessions that took place during the 'Activate Your Abundance' workshop, that was facilitated by Lubna Kharusi, the founder of Dira.

Text in *italics* is the expression and opinion of the individual and is not channeled material.

Channeled Source refers to itself in the channeled sessions as the collective: "We, Us, Our."

Dira International is an organization that offers channeled programs and retreats for people to experience and realize their truth and potential by channeling Divine Source Energy. The vision of Dira is to make a global shift for humanity from separation to Oneness, resulting in the transmutation of the vibration of the world and cosmos.

To find out more about Dira's programs and how you can learn to be a channel visit www.dirainternational.com

C. Intentions

Take a moment to write down your intentions in order to focus your energy and enable the best experience.

D. Liability Waiver

The information provided in this book is for general informational purposes only. The information is not intended to be a substitute for professional health or medical advice or treatment, nor should it be relied upon for the diagnosis, prevention, or treatment of any health consideration. Consult with a licensed health care practitioner before altering or discontinuing any medications, treatment, or care, or starting any diet, exercise or supplementation program. Dira programs and content aim to facilitate an experience of spiritual alignment with the soul and Divine light. They are not a replacement for any other form of therapy, professional advice, medical intervention, or religion, and are only complementary. The by-product of alignment with Divinity through an experience, might enable release, however, we always recommend that one should address any discomfort, be it internal or external, at all levels of their being, including physically, emotionally, mentally, energetically, and spiritually.

2. ABUNDANCE DEFINED

A.   What is Abundance?

Welcome. We are grateful for your presence, and for taking the time to connect. So today, We are going to speak of abundance. In the construct of the human mind, there are many definitions that limit what abundance is. And what We would say is abundance is the allowance of a flow of Divine Vibration. And what does that mean, Divine Vibration? Divine Vibration is not limited to any particular area. It's not limited to love, and it's not limited to strength. And it's not limited to money. It is in that in the infinite attributes of Divine, there is the possibility, by allowing the receiving, through the throat chakra, to have the processing within your energetic field, of all the attributes of Divinity.

And what We would say is, that there are two ways that you can look at it, well there are infinite ways that you can look at it, but from two perspectives is what We will focus on today. The first perspective is that you yourself from your own logical construct decide what it is that you consider that you want to receive. And from the other perspective that you surrender to receiving what is appropriate for you. Starting with the first one, where you have your yearning or desire. There are several variables that affect the possibility of this manifestation. The first variable is the beliefs around whether you are worthy of receiving it. We will give an example, that if a child grows up, and throughout their life, there is the withholding of love so that they perform in a certain way. So for example, you get good grades you get taken to the shop, someone buys you sweets, you get taken to the funfair as a celebration. And when you get bad grades, you're grounded, 'go study some more!'. And so, there is the notion that love is conditional, that flow is conditional.

And this translates to all aspects of life, as love interpermeates everything in existence. And as it interpermeates everything in existence, your beliefs and understanding with regards to love impact everything within your experience. They are the anchoring point for everything. And then you start to grow up a little bit older perhaps, and if your mother or your father has provided a conditioning of how you can receive love, then you start to compound that belief and it ripples to your perception of all forms of receiving love from the community, receiving love from God. Receiving love from yourself. And this worthiness is rippled into your entire experience.

One may say perhaps, how could it be? That all I want to know how to do is, land my perfect job, and then Divine says, first you need to love yourself. Is it conditional on loving yourself? And We would say, you are loved anyway but the opening for receiving is whether you allow it. There is a funnel of connectivity to Divine flow. And you decide through your thoughts and beliefs whether you're going to sip from a cup or whether you're going to swim in the ocean, an infinite ocean that never ends... And has no limitation. It is not that if We love one We cannot love another. It is infinite. But yet with regards to abundance or love, in the construct of the human mind, there tends to be a leaning towards that of scarcity or limitation. And We would say, the only thing that you need to do is open the tap. And how do you open the tap? With your beliefs. Firstly, the belief and knowing that everything that is rooted in Divinity is infinite. And as you are also rooted in Divinity, you are infinite. Does that make sense?

And so then, there is the notion of, what it is that you want to have versus the surrendering to what is possible. And this depends on where one's consciousness sits. Does it sit in the mental body? Or does it sit in the soul? Through your logic, based on prior experience, historical data, your frame of reference, beliefs and conditioning, you decide what is the limitation that you are worthy of. So, for example, if someone were to say to you, here is the lottery ticket, and the prize is five thousand rials, most people would not flinch and say yeah OK, I could possibly win that, why not? But if someone gives you a lottery ticket and say it's 160 million pounds. How many people would truly believe that they're going to win? And then you could say because of the odds. That more people are buying tickets for the 160 million. And We would say, from a logical perspective you assume it has to do with the odds. That is the construct of the mind based on historical data. But from a Divine perspective, anything is possible. And when you step into your Divine space, there is no limit to what is possible. Anything can manifest.

And releasing these limitations or beliefs of what can be received by you, is an area where we will focus today. And so let's say you wake up in the morning, and you go for a walk, or you get dressed and go to work, or you go have breakfast. Is your first thought in the morning: there's no air for me to breathe? It doesn't really enter into the minds of most, unless they have some form of respiratory illness, or they live in a geographical location where the air quality is poor. So, what is it that makes the air quality poor? There is one thing, pollution perhaps. What is the root of pollution? The collective consciousness. When the collective consciousness resists the receiving of Divine vibration, there is an orchestration that reflects that. And so, when you breathe, you breathe in Our love. And when you exhale, We transmute your burdens and release them, through Divine vibration. And so, if you are in a society, or community, or location where it is difficult to breathe, what does that mean? It means that collective consciousness is resisting receiving Divine love.

And you could say that scientifically that makes no sense. They are criteria that prove the cause of it is pollution. And We would say that is the mechanism for the orchestration, it is not the root of the orchestration. And the more people collectively become disconnected from Divine, perhaps one day people will bottle air as they bottled water. Perhaps. But air is an infinite flow of abundance, and its limitation is only the result of the collective consciousness. It is there to enjoy. Same with sunlight, it is a reflection of collective consciousness. Same as the weather systems, they are a reflection of the collective consciousness. They are the signs that We provide for you to turn to the Divine aspect within. And so, in the same way when you believe that you cannot win the 160-million-pound lottery. What is it that formed that limitation? That conditioning? We will do an exercise now, if you like.

B. Exercise 1: Experience Abundance

This exercise is a combination of a core belief release and a throat chakra activation to allow for an expansion of your experience of abundance in physicality.

So just relax. And you're going to focus on the top of your head. There is a luminescent pillar of white light coming down from the sky, it is entering through the top of your head, it is lighting up your body.

And at the heart level, it starts to radiate out of the heart, forming a pyramid of white light around you. And you call on Divine to make itself known to you.

There is a pillar of white luminescent light coming down from the sky it is entering through the top of your head lighting up your body and it starts to radiate out of the heart forming a pyramid of white light around you.

And you call on Divine to make itself known to you. You feel the shift in vibration.

And your crown chakra is becoming larger and larger, and as the crown chakra increases. larger and larger, this pillar of white luminescent light that comes down from the sky is filling this room and it is gushing through you.

The heart becomes larger and larger, opening larger and larger, allowing this river of luminescent white light to flow through you. It gushes in through the top of your head and gushes out through the heart.

So that this entire property is within a pyramid of luminescent white light. There is no confusion that this is the light of Divine. And you feel intensely Our presence.

And then you're going to imagine, that you're going to the center of your heart. The center of your heart it's like a room, and you enter this room, and you feel very comfortable.

You may see a chair or sofa that you sit on and relax. It is very comfortable... And then you're going to get up and walk to the door, and on the count of three when you open the door, you're going to see the person that was a part of your first initial experience where your abundance was limited.

One, two, three! You open the door, and the person walks in the room, or the being walks in the room. And you invite them in.

You may see a scenario or a scene playing. And you may have a conversation with them.

And then next to you, you are going to see the version of yourself when you're that age, standing in front of you on the count of three.

One, two, three! You're standing behind this version of yourself facing the scene of the person, with your arms on the shoulders of this younger version of yourself.

And you're going to receive Divine guidance about the scenario. What is the truth of it? So that this younger version of yourself understands, that it wasn't its fault.

And then you're going to allow the other person in the scene to go away and you're going to face the younger version of yourself, and you look at them with gentle kindness.

And you say it's because of you I understand Divine abundance, and for that I'm grateful'.

THE KEYS TO MANIFESTATION

And you hug this younger version of yourself, and you integrate it into your body, so that you are one.

And once you're integrated, you're going to walk out of the room on the count of three and you're going to see all of the versions of yourself coming from the horizon that held beliefs or constructs that abundance is limited.

One, two, three! You're out of the door and you see on the horizon all of the versions of yourself, that believe that abundance is limited.

The versions of yourself of the past and the versions of yourself in the future all of them are coming towards you.

And you feel from your heart this radiating Divine light, radiating out to all of these versions of yourself, and as they walk towards you, they are consumed by this light that is radiating out of your heart, this Divine light that embraces them and welcomes them and integrates them into you, so that you are all one.

And as they are integrated into you, the beliefs and the limitations are transmuted because this radiating Divine light, demonstrates to them the infinite.

They are all integrated into you. From the past, from the present, and from the future. Transmuted with the Divine light.

And then you're going to walk towards the horizon. And as you walk towards the horizon you will arrive, in the space and the time of your possible existence where you have no limitations of abundance. And you know exactly how it feels to be in this infinite flow.

One, two, three! You're in the time in the space where you're experiencing infinite abundance, and you know how it is, and you know this flow, and you feel what it's like to exist... in a space of receiving Divine vibration in an unlimited form.

And you start to focus on the throat chakra and the throat chakra becomes larger and larger. And as it becomes larger and larger the intensity of this feeling of receiving this infinite Divine abundance is intensifying.

It starts to intensify one thousand times. And you call on this feeling of Divine abundance. It is so clear within you, you can feel this vibration of Divine abundance that is so intense within you and so clear, you know exactly what it is.

You know this is the way it's meant to be.

And as the throat chakra increases even more in size, it becomes larger than this entire property. It is becoming larger and larger and the intensity of this feeling of Divine abundance increases one million times.

You feel this receiving. With no doubt. And you know you are worthy of it. You know that you're connected to it. And at any moment you want to return to this feeling and experience, you can return to it.

And you know with all certainty by sitting in this vibration of receiving infinite Divine abundance, that everything in this universe will be re-orchestrated to ensure the demonstration of this, so that you can physically witness it.

And when you're ready, you come back to your body. Fully present, in this time and space.

3. PERCEPTION & BELIEFS

A. Exercise 2: What do you want?

So, if you would like you can make a list, of the things that you have been thinking about that you want. You take about five minutes to do that. So, you can write it down or maybe you know it very clearly in your head. The things that you want. They can be material or non-material. Take another few moments to complete your list. OK.

B. The Impact of Beliefs on Abundance & Manifestation

Don't worry if you missed something. We know what's in your heart. And We know all your yearnings. But the list has a purpose. For you to understand where you are in your beliefs. Your beliefs about yourself. And your beliefs about your connection to Us. So, as you look at your list, the first thing that you're going to look for, is anything on your list that you believe the Divine is not capable of providing you? Is there anything on your list that We are not able to make happen? And then you're going to look at your list again.

So, what was your answer, is there anything?

Participant 1: *You can provide everything.*

Yes, We can.

And then you're going to look at your list. And you're going to look for anything that you believe that you're not capable of making happen. And you can just circle the ones that you feel, perhaps may not happen. And you're going to tick next to the ones that you are most certain you will make happen. And you will see there will be a sort of grading, or spectrum of those that you have confidence that will occur, or within what you consider within your sphere of influence, and those that you consider are beyond your sphere of influence.

And of those within your sphere of influence, you can also take note of the ones that you believe that you may struggle with, and the ones you believe are effortless. And then of those that are outside your sphere of influence - you're going to look at the ones where you believe that those who are perhaps quote-unquote "responsible to make it happen" will do so because they like you, or because you are good enough, or worthy. And those that you believe that are 'outside of your influence' that you have no option other than just to surrender. And you start to see how the brain compartmentalizes possibility. Where do you put the walls? the dividers? the limitations, on yourself? Because you all said that We can do anything.

So why is it then, that when it comes to you being able to do anything, there are limitations? Is it because you believe you are not a part of Us? Is it because you believe your connection to Us is not strong enough? Is conditional?

ACTIVATE YOUR ABUNDANCE

Would someone like to give some feedback?

Participant 2: *Yes, I feel I am conditioned. I do good I deserve good. I don't do good I don't deserve good.*

So, the belief is that 'God offers that which God sees fit conditionally, depending on whether or not you are good enough'. Any other beliefs?

Participant 3: *I don't deserve it.*

That you don't deserve it because you're not good enough or for another reason?

Participant 3: *Because I am not good enough, I have lost the connection.*

So, the connection is not there? or you're not good enough?

Participant 3: *I am not worthy of it.*

Not worthy.

Participant 4: *Thought processes.*

So thought processes of practicality.

Participant 4: *Logical mind says it's not possible.*

Things that are not possible because based on historical data, the probability is not high enough.

Participant 3: *Who am I to receive this massive amount?*

Who are you to receive? All very common beliefs and constructs.

Participant 3: *Dominant beliefs, patterns, continue in the mind.*

Participant 4: *It is again based on the historical data.*

And what if We were to say that everything on your list is possible if you believe that it is, and the only limitation is the limitation of your mind. To think that that could be true.

Participant 5: *It is also of the construct or beliefs happening from the time relation? When is it going to happen? How is it going to happen?*

Yes, the belief that practicality, indeed. Other beliefs perhaps are similar, 'If I'm not good enough it is that my karma doesn't allow it'.

Participant 4: *Sometimes... for others it is possible, but for me, it's not ok.*

'For others it's OK, but for you it's not OK'.

Participant 4: *Sometimes.*

Or the belief that 'I am too pious to want'.

Participant 5: *Sometimes some spiritual teachings, teach you to slow down your desires. Not to wish anything in order to become a better person, so that's also...*

That 'renunciation, is a path to enlightenment'.

All participants: *Yes.*

THE KEYS TO MANIFESTATION

What do you think? Is that true?

Participant 3: *One of the prophets did that and he got massive abundance.*

What We would say is that what is true for some and not true for others depends on what they believe. If you believe that the only way that you can reach enlightenment is through renunciation, then that is what will manifest, and if you believe that everything in this creation is a gift for you, to aid you, in your enlightenment. And it is there for your enjoyment. Then that will be your path. What does one believe?

And what We would say is that in retrospect, when people look at saints or prophets or sages, and they see that they had no belongings, and they say, for example, they had only a few dates in their store, they had only one item of clothing, they never needed anything. Do you think it's because they were renunciating? or because they had absolute trust in Divine to provide whatever was required whenever needed? They did not need to hoard anything or keep anything because they were connected.

So, in what We would say, the teachings of people who propagate the message that you must relinquish all of the blessings that We have provided you with, We would say that perhaps there isn't that much truth in that or enlightenment. Because being in a space of deprivation is low-frequency vibration and being in a space of Oneness is knowing that you are connected to everything. Everything is blissful and beautiful and Divine and for you to swim in the splendor.

Suffering is a low-frequency vibration and is rooted in fear.

And so, perhaps, the teachers who propagate that you must suffer, have not experienced the bliss of Divine Oneness themselves, because once bliss has been experienced, there is no suffering. One does not need to abstain from everything that has been beautifully provided for you. It is provided for a reason. And you could say perhaps that everything is provided for you to return your conscious awareness to your soul and your light.

And so, when scenarios are presented to you in your external toolkit, they are merely orchestrated for you to understand what it is that you are. A magnificent being of light. And if in your belief system, you believe that to understand that light, you must have no belongings, then that is what will be orchestrated. And if you believe that to understand your light you can enjoy in bliss and splendor, then that is what will be orchestrated. Because Our objective is for you to reach alignment with your magnificent light. Our light that is within you. Not to torture you or make you suffer. But for you to know what We are, and when you know Us, there is no suffering.

Participant 6: *There is a common belief that we have to work really hard to, if you want to say, make money you need to work hard, how it is structured, the harder the job more you get paid, it's very variable. Even in relationships when you want to find a man, you have to get out there. If I have to maintain relationships with friends, I have to make an effort to call. So, yeah, there is a bit of surrender, ok, everything is appropriate, everything will be provided for. There is a feeling that some work needs to be done before*

THE KEYS TO MANIFESTATION

you get something.

So, what We would say is that the way that you are created for this experience to witness your light, is that you have many bodies: a physical body, emotional, mental, egoic, astral, and soul. They are your toolkit. And so, for example in the action, the ego is that tool that enables inertia or action. If it is dominant, then it suppresses the soul, and if it is in balance, it enables an action that is the result of your inner guidance. And your inner guidance is not controlling. Your inner guidance doesn't want you to suffer. Your inner guidance doesn't want you to stay in bad relationships. Your inner guidance will use the ego to enable the taking of action so that things may manifest. But in that action, there should be bliss. It should not feel like it's an effort, and when an effort is exerted, it's because your focus is on the wrong place. It shouldn't be difficult; it should be blissful.

So, no pain no gain, is a construct. And a belief system that some people resonate with, and others don't. Is it the criteria for things to unfold and manifest? No. Can it be a root for it to unfold and manifest? If your belief is that you must suffer to gain anything, then that is what your experience will be. And if your belief is that everything will be handed to you on a beautiful platter with flowers and birds singing, that is what will come to you. It is not that you take no action, it is that the action that you take is rooted and guided by your inner guidance. But when you take action that is not coming from the space of the soul's instruction, that action is superfluous. And it's just a diversion.

Participant 3: *So, will I be guided?*

You are guided, but are you listening?

So, for example, someone has a number of job options, as an example, one is paying ten times the salary of the other. So, for example, you are a musician, you can be a musician and earn one hundred dollars a week, or you could be an accountant and earn ten thousand dollars a week, for example. You love music, you hate accountancy, but because of your fear, which is not from the soul's knowing, your fear is in the root chakra, you want security, and you say, 'OK I will take the accountancy job for ten thousand dollars because that way my fear is covered'. I just mask my fear, I don't deal with it, but I mask it. And so, the fear continues, it never goes away and you are the prisoner of your fear. Whereas if you took the musician role where you earn perhaps a hundred dollars a week, because it's the guidance of the soul, the soul knows what your magnificent possibility is, you might become the next superstar. Or you might not become the next superstar, but you will be happy.

And which is more important? When you're in a space of happiness, bliss and gratitude, abundance flows infinitely. And when you're disgruntled and miserable you will always be feeling uncomfortable. You might have a bigger paycheck, but in actuality, you are depriving yourself of the magnificent possibility, of surrendering to Our orchestration of perfection by exercising your free will and stepping down from the possibility that We offer you. And why would anyone do that? Because they don't know the future, but We do. We know everything because everything has already happened in its infinite possibilities, and so you decide how you're going to hop between these options.

THE KEYS TO MANIFESTATION

Participant 3: *How can I listen?*

Well, you know how to channel now, you make it to part of the way that you live. And you don't do anything that is not a result of your inner guidance, let go of the fear of 'How am I going to pay my bills'. Fear is not that which enables abundance, it blocks it. Gratitude is what enables abundance. And so, for the musician, they have a choice, perhaps they could say because in their mental construct, they say 'Practically I can afford to become a musician after a year of me working for ten thousand dollars a week as an accountant. I'm willing to suffer for a year. And then I'll have my savings ready. And then I can be me, but I'm putting off being me until I've covered my fear'. Then it's practical.

Are We saying that everyone should just leave their miserable jobs? No, what We're saying is that deal with your fears and then you can sit in discomfort for less time. Because the fear that you must have this income is rooted in the notion that We are not an infinite provider. And what We would say is that in the surrendering, you might not have the fixed salary that comes in every week or every month, but you will have abundant flow in other ways, ways that you couldn't have imagined using your logic.

Participant 3: *Massive abundance.*

Abundance that is appropriate to your belief system. So, if you believe it will be massive, We will accommodate massiveness. But what We would also say, is that in the cleansing of your system of frequency, the desire for massive, half massive, or less massive, becomes irrelevant, it is the trusting that you are held in a Divine embrace and the Divine embrace is the most appropriate for your purpose in your existence, which is to understand your light.

Participant 3: *I have a pain in my solar plexus.*

Because the ego would like massive and why would the ego like massive. To feel loved. If you are successful people will see you and love you more.

Participant 3: *I don't get this; can you give an example?*

It means you will be accepted; you will be validated. Then you are worthy of love. And it's OK. Most people feel that way, why does someone want a fancy car? Because they want people to love them. They assume that love comes from the validation through external symbology, I have a nice car, I have nice clothes, I have a beautiful house. And this makes me lovable. When you love yourself. Everyone loves you anyway. Because they are Our messengers. They are the reflection to you of your state of conscious awareness. And if you feel that people outside of you are not showing you love, it is just the messenger to say, 'Why aren't you loving yourself?', what they say is not important, what is important is the software that you play in your head. 'When I get this job, I'm OK, when I have this car, I'm OK'.

Participant 7: *Is it that, we are kidding ourselves when we say, I want this house for myself? I want this nice house because I want to feel good, I don't care what people will think, I just want it because I like it!*

Yes, of course, that is possible. That is of course possible and there is nothing wrong with enjoying the beautiful gifts that We offer. What we're saying is the intention that drives action if it is from a place of fear or insecurity, or not feeling enough, or not loving yourself. Then address the core issues first. But if you're already in a space of self-love and trust and Divine and fearless. then there is nothing that would stop you from enjoying the splendor of this creation, and the splendor includes beautiful homes, and in your beautiful home, you share your love with others.

Participant 6: *Then it looks like, if we are balanced and aligned and if we are in the process of intending desires which result in being manifested, it's one of the most important purposes of existence, in creation.*

Yes. But when the launch of intent, We will speak now about how manifestation occurs. And as you mentioned, what is the purpose of this existence? So, the purpose of this existence is to understand and witness and experience Divinity.

If you were to imagine that the Divine is a vacuum, and once witnessed it lights up. It lights up as a white light, but beyond the white light that has been known or experienced or is in the process of being experienced. There is also an infinite vacuum. As there is infinite light. And so, in the human construct, the notion of that which is infinite is infinite, cannot be beyond that there is even beyond infinite. Beyond infinite of infinite. It's just not quite comprehensible for the brain.

Participant 6: *So Divine is this consciousness in a vacuum?*

Yes. And so, this white light yearns to be experienced and witnessed, and so it refracts into a spectrum of color, which are your souls that come to a physical realm to be witnessed and experienced. And when you are in this experience everything in your external experience is merely a mirror of whether this refracted spectrum of color that you are, is being witnessed or not. And so, if it's not being witnessed then the scenario becomes uncomfortable, and if it is being witnessed then the scenario is very comfortable and blissful.

So, whenever things are happening in your life that you feel uncomfortable about, then you can know with all certainty that you are not aligned with your soul's vibration in your thoughts. What does that mean? it means your thoughts contradict what the soul knows is true. And until you shift your thoughts, you will continue in discomfort because the soul is very clear. It wants to be experienced and witnessed and it will persist creating this discomfort until you acknowledge the truth of what it is and can witness it accurately. And how does the soul influence your external environment? Through the heart and through the vibration of love.

Love interpermeates everything in existence and through your heart there is a sort of extension to the external environment. You perceive it as an external environment, but it of course connected to you through the vibration of love, or golden light, that interpermeates everything in creation. And so, as you project out you could say thoughts that you hold, they are influencing through the heart this network of golden light, influencing the universe and so the universe is reorchestrated by Divine Source energy to ensure that it matches the pulses that you have been emitting. So that the entire universe reflects exactly what it is that your thoughts are and what the most appropriate scenario will be orchestrated to reflect to you the alignment or disalignment between your thoughts and your soul.

So, it is not only that your thoughts create reality, but also the alignment or disalignment between your thoughts and what the soul knows is true. So, your thought maybe, 'I'm going to have this amazing car, I am going to have this amazing car, I'm going to have this amazing car'. But underlying it the dominant thought is, 'Unless I have this amazing car, I'm not cool, no one is going to love me'. And the soul knows that you will be loved. But the soul is not being witnessed as long as you have this underlying thought of 'Nobody's going to love me unless I have this car'.

And so, what happens, through the heart, there is a projection outward that orchestrates the scenario that shows you that you are not loved. It might not be that you don't get the car, you might get the car. But what is being projected out is that you are not loved. So, you get the amazing car and then you have a huge fight with your best friend, as an example. And you say that 'I got an amazing car, I thought that would make me loveable, my friend is not impressed with me, isn't loving me'. Because what was emitted out is not the fault of the car, what is emitted out is that 'I am not loved'.

And so, the soul is saying 'What would be the best scenario for them to realize that even if they have this car, they are not going to be loved because of it'. They need to have a scenario where they realize that the car is not going to be what makes them loved. It is that they have to love themselves. And so, you keep having these repetitive patterns that continue with this underlying feeling of conditional love. Conditional love of things, that things are what makes your love conditional, conditional love of your actions, etc. And so, the scenarios continue to play until you can shift the underlying thought that love is conditional. Does that make sense? So, the root thought or the root belief is what dominates the manifestation.

You may have the sub-thought which is, 'I need a car', realized as a reinforcement for you to understand the dominant thought which is: love is conditional. Or you may have a different scenario, you don't get the car, and then you still discover that you are loved regardless. So, you don't get the car, and everyone is still your friend. And you tell your friends, 'Look I cannot afford it, I'm not as rich as you thought.' And they say, 'We still love you'. So, the realization can come in alternate routes which is the most appropriate route for you is the one that will manifest. But everything that manifests is for you to understand whether your beliefs and thoughts are aligned with what the soul knows is true. And We orchestrate that, as the Supreme Omnipotent, Omniscient.

C. Perspective & Manifestation

Participant 8: *Can you explain how can we adjust how our soul assumes things? Like this unconditional love. If you have already experienced all throughout your life and that's what your soul is reflecting, that you don't get the car then you are not worthy of this love. That's how it's always been, and you know that's the relationship has always been. It's clearly stated on daily basis, so there's nothing that has changed. So, you know what I mean. How to handle this?*

So, you do a resolution. So, in the same way that you did the resolution earlier about abundance, you do the resolution about how love is unconditional. And you reintegrate the parts of you that split off in the belief that love is conditional, through channel. So, the exercise would be, that you are in channel, and then you bring the versions of yourself where you believed that love was conditional. You have a resolution through channel, and you integrate that energy back into it. And then the belief that love is conditional no longer persists with you because all the moments of your existence where it was diverging from the truth, that love is unconditional, are brought back to the knowing that it is unconditional. OK?

Participant 5: *Is the resolution important? Isn't it easier just to change the thought patterns day to day?*

So changing your thought pattern assumes that you have control over the subconscious mind. And the subconscious mind is dominant over the conscious. So, you could say that with beliefs and perceptions, the way that the functionality of the mental body is always continuously looking for reinforcement of the beliefs from the subconscious perspective. So, it's like the drawing up of all that is in the subconscious is merely to reconfirm those dominant beliefs, and so there is a struggle that you will face if you try to do it from a mental perspective. You do it at an energetic level first and then at a conscious level you can follow through consciously looking for the reconfirmation of that which has been resolved and released. But to assume that you only function in the brain is limited. You function at all levels. And so that which is a belief that you hold for example is stored in every cell of your being. And it is stored in all the infinite chakras that you have.

And so, if you are to say that I am only going to address this at the mental-body level, although it may have an effect for some time, it is not a full resolution that is in the holistic embrace, because they are parts of you that you're not aware that still store this data. And people assume that the imprints that they have can just disappear because they've decided it's going to disappear. The imprints that you leave behind are there for eternity unless they are transmuted energetically. So, for example every place that you walk, every thought that you have, is a form of consciousness, you could consider it like a ball of consciousness that has been programmed. And it floats till eternity in existence. And so how do you gather all these balls just using your brain? It doesn't happen. It happens at one level. But if you wanted to transmute, it needs to happen energetically first.

Participant 6: *So, we first transmute and then still as thoughts create reality and we want to create beautiful reality around us. Do we still do positive affirmations?*

You can, yes.

Participant 6: *In the morning to affect our well-being?*

Yes.

Participant 6: *Then, if you feel a good thought, so your body resonates, and it produces good emotions. And the body heals the cell memory that has been stored there before, isn't so?*

Eventually so. But if you want to resolve it, in an instant, you do a resolution energetically through channel. We know what we're doing. Perhaps We know more than the brain does. Considering We created the brain. And know its limitations. Anso, what We would say is that, yes, there is this co-creative notion that has presented. That you are powerful infinite beings that through your thought projection you can create a reality and what We would say is that is not the full picture. It is true to a degree, and it is true because We accommodate your thoughts. But will your thoughts override the Divine plan? No! And perhaps that makes some uncomfortable. And what We would say is that, in connection and Oneness there is no separation between Us and you. And so, at a level or perspective, you could say that you are all powerful and can also orchestrate the universe because you are Us, in a perspective. But in the perspective of the dual realm, which is where you exist in your dominant state, most sit within the ego, or the sex chakra, and few in the heart. And if you are in the projective notion from the sex chakra vibration, or the ego vibration of the solar plexus, to assume that that lower frequency of vibration of manifestation will override the vibration of Oneness in its will, then that is a delusion.

So, if you are in the space of Oneness, then indeed the manifestation of which is projected through you, through your thoughts is aligned with Divine Will if you project through the Ajna or through the crown. If you project through the Ajna, then it is aligned with your soul as refracted light but still Divine Will, will override it because your spectrum of refracted light is a subservient component to that which is white light. And so, then you imagine, the frequency goes further and is in the solar plexus, which is where most of the collective consciousness sits. And therefore, so much projection is from the place of the ego or the personality 'How does this define me, I make my beautiful vision board, I have my car, I have my house, I have my dog, I have my kids, I have the wedding ring, I have the wedding dress'. And in this projection, you want all of these amazing things not fully conscious of why. Aside from, that you think it will make you feel better.

Whereas from the Divine perspective of Oneness, we know exactly why you want it. We know you want it to be loved, to feel connected and to reach Oneness. We also know how the most perfect way to orchestrate the attainment of Oneness or the experience of unconditional love. And so, We might accommodate these desires, of the car, of the house, and the ring, and the dress. And We might not. Our Will is what overrides because the frequency of vibration is of a higher spectrum than that of the spectrum of color yellow in the solar plexus. And especially because not only is the solar plexus a lower spectrum of vibration than Oneness. It is also usually contaminated with even lower spectrum of vibration such as red, because of fear. So it is not in arrogance that We say that 'Divine Will' overrides 'individualized will', because as long as you are in a state of duality and a state of separation, and you believe that there is an 'I', that frequency of which you are existing in, is subservient to the collective white light. Does that make sense?

And so, We would say perhaps that there has been a misrepresentation in the dissemination of information and marketing to in a positive view to empower people to take responsibility for their life and to have the confidence that they can do things. And from a perspective, it has reason to be experienced and witnessed. But perhaps now there is need for transmutation and expansion of awareness, to know that it is in the state of Oneness that manifestation occurs in an instant, and the entire universe can be re-orchestrated through you when you are in a state of Oneness. But as long as you are in the ego or anything that is of spectra of vibration that is refracted, Divine Will will override it.

Participant 1: *Can you give an example?*

For example, We will make it simple. You have your car on your vision board, you focus on it every day, you know it's going to come. You feel it, can smell the leather in the car, it is so real for you already. It's so real. And then you're going to the showroom. You pay the money for the car and you're going to collect the keys on the way there. There's a hurricane. And the showroom is flooded. No more car. The company goes bankrupt. That kind of car doesn't exist anymore. So yes, your desire has been accommodated. But Our Will, will overrule it. For whatever reason would be appropriate. And maybe it's to see that, I was so close to getting it. So close to being validated. And then this natural disaster occurs. And things are put in perspective, what's a car after all? 'Do I need it when people are dying? And there is suffering, and people lose their homes. And as a community, we come together to help one another? And as a community, we come together and take people into our homes who no longer have one. And we show them love, unconditional love.' And then you know that unconditional love exists. You don't need a car. Does that make sense?

Participant 1: *But from the point of the Divine - Divine can do anything for us, we deserve it.*

Capable of doing anything for you and?

Participant 1: *I deserve to have a car, let's say a I deserve to have a Mercedes for example. Not because I need it, but because I deserve it and I like it.*

What does 'deserve' mean?

Participant 1: *To be worthy of it.*

To be worthy of it. You are worthy of this whole universe and hence it has been given to you. Every morning you breathe the air, and you walk outside in the sun shines on your skin. And in the nighttime, you look up to the sky and you see stars and their constellation. And perhaps you walk to the beach, and you watch the sunset, and you see the sea, and you see how everything in the ocean is in its perfect orchestration, and that every grain of sand on the beach is uniquely diverse, just like every soul is uniquely diverse. And as the breeze blows on you it is us loving you. And in the garden, the birds chirp. And then your baby comes running to you saying 'Mommy!' and hugs you. Is that not loving you? Are you not worthy of that? And which is more important the car or the universe that is provided to you?

Participant 8: *But I still haven't got the car!*

And We would say, the car will manifest instantaneously when the yearning for the car is in the spectrum of the crown of Oneness, but when they are yearning for the cars in the root chakra for example rooted in fear. The fear will be addressed first.

Participant 6: *Put it in the crown!*

Participants: *That is so beautiful! It makes so much sense.*

So, We will explain this. We were discussing earlier about the white light and the refraction. And so, Divine in itself is also expanding, and how does that expansion occur? through the experiencing and witnessing of Us. As this light starts to be witnessed, it lights up. So, in the tapestry of the Divine, the lights light up within this vacuum. And how is it they light up? They light up through your witnessing of Us. And then in the shadow of Us, there is the yearning to see the Divinity. So, the yearning to have love for example. But then you would say love is A, B, C. But could love not be the entire alphabet? It's just so far you have witnessed A, B, C. But love also is beyond the A, B, C. Infinitely beyond the A.B.C. And so, then is this yearning to experience different types of love.

The first love you experienced with your mother is an example. And then you perhaps experience a form of romantic love, love in the community, self-love. Different forms of love, love of nature, love of your own children. Always continuously evolving. And so, once it has been experienced does the experiencing just stop and you get bored and you think, 'Ah, I know everything about love, nothing left to know, seen it all.' Or is there a yearning to have more? You taste something. You see the stranger across the road and there is an instant connection when you look into each other's eyes and there is this yearning for something more, of what could this be? and so you launch this intent. You launch the intent from the space of gratitude of the heart, like a ball.

There is this projectile, and you can visualize now, that in you, you see this stranger across the road your eyes meet and there is this yearning inside to experience more. And you're grateful for that split second where your eyes connected. And so, this ball comes out of the heart in the vibration of gratitude and is projected out. It is projected out for manifestation. And so, what maintains this ball in the air? Gratitude or any frequency of gratitude higher than gratitude. So, when you project intention from the level of the heart, the throat, the Ajna, or the crown the ball is lifted and held in a high vibration to ensure its manifestation. Does that make sense so far? We will change the scenario a bit. You see someone, and the same person, later you see them across the road. And then this fear comes in, 'Oh, my gosh he's going to like me' and you're in fear, 'Oh I hope he likes me, he's so cute! But I don't think he's going to like me, nobody likes me'. And then you're like, 'But I want to know more'. And you throw this ball - plop! And the launch just kind of plonks down because the vibration is not elevated enough to keep it suspended for manifestation. You launch it and plonk it goes, because the projectile within which it is projected is not of a sustainable frequency. And so when you try to manifest through fear it usually just plonks down. And then you say, 'See, God doesn't listen to me. I've been forsaken and abandoned. Or I'm not worthy of having my prayers listened to'.

That has nothing to do with Us not wanting to listen, it's that it didn't reach because the vibration in which it was projected was too low of a frequency to sustain it. In the same way, your monthly bills come in. And you're in fear 'I'm not going to meet my commitments', and then you start playing in your head. I'm going to get the bailiff coming after me. I'm going to lose my apartment. My wife is going to start screaming at me. And you're in the fear of 'I can't meet my commitments'. But I want money, I'm launching intention. I know it's going to rain sunshine, but it's in fear, so goes plonk. Whereas if it is launched from the space of gratitude to a higher vibration, from the space of 'I know I'm taken care of, and I have absolute trust and I'm so grateful that I'm always taken care of. And I know that as soon as I walk outside and I feel the air on my face, and I am completely embraced in Divine love. There's nothing to worry about, because I surrender, and I don't need to think about how it's going to happen, but I know with all certainty it will. Because I trust and I'm grateful for the Divine love I experience every day.' Do you see the difference? It is - what frequency of vibration is this yearning expressed? And We are aware of all the yearnings that you have. But from Our perspective, the yearning that is dominant is what takes precedence. And so, if the yearning is to let go of your fear as opposed to getting the bills paid.

First, We will address letting go of fear because that is for the transmutation and alignment of the soul. And the purpose of your existence is for the alignment with your Divine magnificence. It is not to get your bills paid or have a car, that is secondary. The purpose of this existence is to witness the Divine. And anything that stands in the way of witnessing the Divine such as fear, frustration, or anger, will be dealt with first. Does that make sense? And it is not to make you suffer. It is for you to be One with Us. If you believe you need to suffer, We will accommodate that belief as long as it brings you to Us. Because you came from Us, and you will return to Us, in Oneness. And even though for a moment in time, you are refracted spectrum in duality, you will return to Us, in Oneness.

Participant 6: *So basically, to feel fear is fine, it's just the key for you to pay attention and work with it?*

Yes. Everything is fine. In the end, you choose how you want to experience this existence. You can linger in fear all the time. Or you can transmute that vibration to a higher spectrum of vibration. So, for example, you're in a relationship and your partner cheats on you. Rage arises and what is this rage? The rage is this 'What does this make me? I'm not good enough, I'm not lovable, what does it make me?'. You projected it as they are evil. 'How dare they?'. But what upsets you and causes this rage is in the solar plexus. It is 'How am I now defined? How can I accept someone like that? What does it make me if I accept this behavior? How does it define me? Am I now not enough that they must go elsewhere? Am I not lovable enough?'. And so, this rage stirs in you, and you can sit in this rage for twenty years or you can let it go in ten minutes, it's up to you. And how do you let it go? You transmute it because in the solar plexus, there is freedom as well. And so, you can sit in this rage, or you move into freedom which then transmutes it to the heart, where you are in a space of acceptance.

Acceptance that, 'The person in front of me who cheated on me, has the same underlying vibration that I have'. The belief that they are not enough and that they are not loved and hence they cheat. And the only reason why the two of you came into the scenario together in this experience, is because your frequency and root belief are the same, that 'I'm not enough and I'm not loved'. How is this expressed? One expresses it through cheating, and in the other, it is expressed through the anger of the scenario. But you all came together because the belief is the same. And then there is the third party, who also was in the scenario, who was cheated with. And then someone would say 'Family wrecker! How dare they come into my marriage?'. But that person is exactly the same as you, who believed that they are not enough and not loved and hence they accept to be with someone unavailable.

Participant 1: *So, the vibration is sent out from us?*

Yes. And as the vibration is sent out through you, to this external, you could consider it's not external, it is a part of you, it is an extension of you, and hence everything in this extension is vibrating at the resonating frequency to you. And so, you have the mistress and you have the cheating husband. They hold the same frequency of underlying belief as you. They believe too, they are not enough, and they believe too that they are not loved. And when you reach a point of Oneness, of the understanding that their pain is as painful as your pain. Then you can let it go. But as long as there is this notion of separation, that 'They did this, and I am different. I would never do that.' And what We would say is that you have done everything. In Oneness, you have been everything, you are everything and you are them. There is the illusion, that your skin separates you from them, but they are you, and you are them. Because you are Us. And We interpermeate everything in Divine love.

Participant 6: *So then in the scenario that you gave us what is the best solution to change the vibration and get out of the situation? You accept it, forgive everyone and you move on with your life?*

So, then you will end up in the next relationship where you also get cheated on because you have not addressed the issue of 'I am not enough, and I am not lovable'. And therefore, everything in your extension of experience will reflect that back to you until that belief is released. And so, you go back to the root event of your life, where that belief was formed, and you release it. And then you take all of the events of your life that reconfirmed that belief and release

THE KEYS TO MANIFESTATION

them. And you reintegrate all of the parts of you that split off in this pain of not being enough and not being lovable. And you transmute through channel. and reintegrate them back into you, so that you are whole lovable and enough.

Participant 6: *Do we have the power to understand that the problem is not cheating, but it is about loving myself? How do I know that I understand that is the problem?*

You channel, so you will always have the appropriate guidance in channel, and if you ask why is this happening? You will be given the answer. It is never about the other because there is no other! They are the extension of you, perhaps the face looks different. So then just ignore their face and put your face on their head. They are the extension of you, and from an energetic perspective, you are continuing into them. And all of the resonating frequency of vibration is what is in your experience. So, you may have all those amazing guys who don't cheat - why are they not with you? because they are not in your resonance.

Participant 6: *Is there an amazing guy who doesn't cheat?*

Most certainly!

Participant 2: *We have here.*

Participant 1: *So, it is our belief that men are cheaters? Are there good honest men out there?*

Of course.

Participant 1: *I want one!*

And what We would say is it's not about the guy.

Participant 1: *It's about loving ourselves unconditionally and accepting ourselves.*

And then when you are at that resonance of frequency, of anything that is higher than the heart chakra, so any frequency above the heart chakra, is in the vibration for the manifestation of blissful experience. And that which is the lower frequency than the heart chakra is vibration for the manifestation of uncomfortable experience. So, when you stay in a place of love or gratitude, acceptance, Oneness, and connectivity, your experience becomes reflective of that vibration. And is it that you will be in a constant state your entire life? No. There is fluctuation because you are a dynamic being. But it is to hold conscious awareness enough that in every moment of your existence, you are aware. Here is a story: The monk goes to the airport, the flight is delayed, then he sits calmly and meditates. And then it's twenty-two hours later and the flight still isn't taking off and he sits patiently and meditates. Some forty-eight hours pass. Six weeks pass and he's still at the airport.

There will be moments where he will think 'What's going on?!'. Just because he's a monk, and can maintain a certain vibration, does that mean they're not blips or moments of lapse? Of course, they are. So, you don't say that 'I'm not good enough' if I have a moment of fear, or if I have a moment of anger, or a day of anger even. There is no harm in that. The harm comes when you sit in it, and it becomes your dominant vibration. So, you can be angry, let it go. And ten minutes later, the morning later, the day later, you've let it go. But if you sit in it for twenty years, you're depriving humanity of experiencing an aspect of the Divine that can only be experienced through you. So why do it? Firstly, it's uncomfortable for you, and secondly, We want to be witnessed. And you have been chosen as Our vice regent. Right? So, do you eliminate anger? Or do you eliminate fear? Or do you eliminate ego? No, you have been given tools and all of the spectrum of vibration is part of the tool, and in duality, the spectrum of vibration has a dual opposite. So, there is fear and security: they are dual opposites, both are valid, both are important for the witnessing. But how long you sit in discomfort is up to you, that is your free will. The soul is giving you the signals. It's making you uncomfortable. And you can choose to ignore it as long as you like. The more you ignore it, the stronger the signal.

Participant 1: *We should be addressing it and releasing it?*

Yes, continuously.

Participant 1: *As it comes?*

Yes. And you will see for yourself that the time period for you which you sit in low vibratory spectrum becomes less and less. And how free are you going to be when you're not in the shackles of fear and pain and guilt and shame and anger. You imprison yourselves; you are imprisoning your soul from shining. That is the exercising of free will. The experience will be orchestrated and how you choose to view that experience is your free will. Does that make sense? Are you going to change the hurricane from happening? No. But how you experience that hurricane is up to you. You can sit with your children, and you marvel in awe at the rain, or you can sit with your children in fear hiding under the couch, that you're going to be doomed. And it's up to you, one experience is more blissful than the other. The event is identical. But how you experience it, is your choice. And so, you can elevate your spectrum of vibration so that it is a blissful experience. Or you can reduce it so that it is not blissful. OK? We will take a break. Thank you.

D. Poem: Wild Abundance

'Nearby the lake, a cry from the loon
That pierces the silence below the rising moon.
A ripple through the water as a fish jumps up;
The loon calls over his friends to try their luck.

And the fog starts to settle above the lake.
The animals, so careful in every move that they make
For their life, they think, is what is at stake
But only that which is planned is what We will take.

And the berries grow on a prickly hedge,

A risk for the deer who go to fetch,
But that sweetness is worth it, it's worth every scratch
And they are grateful for the bountiful batch.

The provision that is given for each and every being,
Before you receive it, may not be seen,
But all is apportioned in appropriate time
And it flows to you freely when you are aligned.

The beaver collects twigs to build his dam
And the fox observes; he is a fan.
But yet this beaver is an example for common man
Of how building your dream concurs with Our plan.

When you sit back and observe the creatures of the wild,
They have more knowledge than any adult or child;
They understand the flow of Our provision
As all division is under Our supervision.

And humans, out of breath, worry and pace,
Thinking provisions comes from a race.
It is gratitude that allows abundance to flow:
So simple a formula for you to know.
Though gratitude seems so difficult to feel
And in the panic of lack, you grab or you steal.
Whereas if you knew there is enough for all
Our blessings would flow whenever you call.

Thank you.'

4. THE VIBRATION FOR MANIFESTATION

A. Surrender & Trust in Divine

So, We will continue. Depending on the frequency with which there is a launch of intention or desire or yearning, is what will take precedence. And so, for example, as We had mentioned at the beginning, there are two possible perspectives that We will be discussing: the first is where you decide what is good for you and what you need. And the second is We decide, and you surrender to that.

So now that you understand, that based on the frequency of where you launch this intention from, offers the propelling force for it to happen. And if you are sitting in the root chakra frequency, or sex chakra frequency, or solar plexus frequency, it does not have full momentum to be launched. Then most certainly that which is of a higher frequency vibration will take precedence over it. And then to continue on, if it is in a higher frequency vibration, the frequency at the Ajna chakra is that the intention is aligned with the soul's yearning, and the frequency of the crown chakra is in the frequency of Oneness is that the intention is aligned with Divine Will. And so, yes you can go through your life, gambling you could call it, in that there is the possibility that perhaps your intention is aligned with the higher frequency of the Divine Will or the soul. Or it could be aligned with your solar plexus such as the ego, or your desires in the sex chakra. But you're gambling because you're not consciously aligned necessarily with where this intention is coming from. If you are aligned with where the intention is coming from, then you wouldn't launch intentions that were not at the frequency of Ajna or the crown.

And so, when We say, that there is the other option of just surrendering to Divine Will and orchestration, it takes out all of the effort on your part. Because even if your intention from your perspective is aligned with the Ajna, or the crown, there is still the possibility that you are limiting its magnificence. Because you perhaps would say, 'I want a beautiful home.' And you have a picture of it in your mind or in a magazine of what this beautiful home looks like, but perhaps the magnificent possibility is something far more splendid. Maybe you want a car and perhaps the magnificent possibility is a private jet. So, you are limiting yourself by deliberate expression of intention from the mental body because the mental body is limited to that which it deems possible based on historical data collection.

And so, for example, let's say that your child is about to go to university. And you see your child, you know that their gift is that they are extremely nurturing, as an example. And you say, 'Perhaps for them to be a doctor or a veterinarian so that they can express this nurturing aspect would be aligned with their soul's vibration, and so you launch intention that this is possible. And you convince them that this is the best route for them and then they launch the intention. Because even if you launch your intention for someone else, it's only when they launch it that it is accommodated. So, then they launch this intention, 'I want to be a doctor'. And even though it is aligned with the soul's vibration, and aligned with Divine vibration, is that the most magnificent possible outcome for them? It enables them to shine in their nurturing Divinity, but do they shine the most magnificently that they could?

For example, maybe instead of a doctor, they could be a world-renowned healer, that heals millions of people. Through the work or the education platform that they provide. And so therefore they can shine in their light more. And what We mean by shining the light more, is that there is a further radiance of the light and its impact on humanity. And its impact and the possibility of that spectrum of Divine to be witnessed by a greater sphere. And as the sphere expands in its radiance, the intensity of that vibration compounds, and so perhaps before they were born the understanding of nurturing was A, B, C. And by the time they die, from a collective consciousness perspective, their understanding of nurturing is from A to Z. Whereas if they were a doctor, which is also aligned with this Divine aspect of nurturing, they got to only F.

So, in the projection of intention of being too specific, as opposed to surrendering to Divine's magnificent plan for you, there is a limitation. Again, We refer to this as through the exercising of 'free will' you are stepping down from magnificence. And in the trust and surrender, that Divine provides the most magnificent circumstance for the full witnessing of the soul. And what does enlightenment refer to? If not that there is an absolute alignment with the soul so that this radiant light can shine infinitely. Does that make sense?

Participant 1: *How can I witness the alignment of my soul to the Divine magnificence?*

By surrendering to what is presented to you and not resisting it. So, for example, you're in a marriage, and this marriage is very uncomfortable, but you persist in it. Unwilling to see the signs of this discomfort. And then you develop breast cancer. And you start to reflect on your life, and you think 'If I live through this, I owe it to myself to not continue in misery'. So, you had left it to the point of a fatal illness before there was the conscious awareness that it was uncomfortable and not aligned with your soul. Whereas, it is possible, before even being married that when you see the person, you know is this right or not, isn't it?

Participant 1: *I made a mistake.*

It is not that it is a mistake. It is how long one chooses to linger in discomfort. Because the discomfort arises to highlight to you that you have a thought frequency not aligned with the soul. And so, the discomfort has purpose, and making that 'mistake', which is not a mistake, it is the appropriate decision in that moment and time. To go in a pathway and enter a scenario that highlights to you that 'What it is that I think is not reflective of what my soul knows is true?'. So, you enter into the marriage thinking this is the best I can get, someone who beats me, as an example.

Participant 1: *I was hearing the voice of the soul asking me to leave that relationship. To leave that marriage, but I ignored it, till it came to this point where I could not ignore it.*

Exactly, and then you realize 'I'm worthy of more. And I deserve love. Because I am love'. And so, there is a surrendering, because in the exercising of free will you latch on and you say, 'I am not going to fail at my marriage, because people who get   divorced are failures and I am not one of them'. Or 'It takes strength to be in an unhappy marriage and I am very strong'. Assuming that strength is from the endurance of misery. Whereas if you look at attribute from a Divine perspective, We are not miserable and We are the most Infinite Strength. And so, it is the construct of the mind that defines how you want to be and how you choose to define yourself, and then those definitions are not aligned with that the knows to be true, you're only putting yourself in suffering. We do not make you suffer. You do that to yourselves.

We will repeat that. We do not make you suffer. You do that to yourselves. You also decide how long you're going to suffer. Because there is the possibility to transmute a vibration instantly. And then you would say perhaps, 'How is it that you can say that we do not make people suffer, when there are people starving in the world?'. And We would say you assume that they suffer because they don't have the presentation of wealth that you assume brings happiness. But perhaps they are more connected to Us, than the richest man in the world. Perhaps. Perhaps, they do not see it as suffering unless they believe that it should be different. And the soul knows that whatever is presented is most perfect. So, you say that there is suffering, but you assume that they think and have the same beliefs that you do. Can't very wealthy people suffer far more because of the disconnection? Suffering is rooted in disconnection from Divine. And in connection, there is no suffering regardless of the presentation of circumstance.

Because even if in the environment, it looks like it is a desperate scenario. The reality is that, as human beings, your existence is about relationships. And so, people fall in love even if they're hungry. And they make connections, and they love their children, and they love their parents, and they're part of a community. And they may for example, at the moment there is a refugee situation. There is the propaganda that creates more suffering, in the highlighting of how they should be so unhappy, that if there wasn't the imposition of certain beliefs, many would get on with it and fall in love and go about their day and survive. But when there is the constant reminder that you must be miserable, and suffer more, then they do suffer more. But it is not because of their experience or surroundings, it is because there is a disconnection and the implantation of fear that causes the lack of trust in Divine orchestration.

Does that make sense? How many have watched a movie about war? And the movie is about a love story? The war becomes the background scene, but your individualized experience is about the expression of your soul. The backdrop is the war, but the foreground is your story. If the person you saw across the street, or your eyes met, and something clicked. Or the first time you see your child. You can take a scenario of currently, in Oman, where there is the notion that the oil price was very low, and there was a concern about the funding for the country, how many people took any notice? That problem was looming, building, there, very present, but it affects how much of your day. Did it affect your every moment of your day? Or is it perhaps something that you think of when you're in a meeting, or you have a conversation, or you watch the news? Your every day is about enjoying simple pleasures.

It's about waking up, having your breakfast, greeting the people you love, getting dressed, taking a shower, perhaps going to work or not. Doing whatever it is that is in your day-to-day routine that is the culmination of simple pleasures.

And then you have one incident, the guy next to you at the traffic light, tries to cut you off, and your entire day is doomed, because of a split-second incident. And the other twenty-three hours and fifty-nine minutes and thirty-three seconds were beautifully blissful, but you focus on that twenty-second incident at the traffic light. And say, 'I had such a terrible day, you won't believe what happened!'. So, where you choose to sit in your vibration is up to you. You can restrain that frustration to the thirty seconds after the incident, or you can spend all week moaning about it. You choose to suffer, We don't make suffering. And why did that incident occur in the first place? It's just reflecting to you whether that behavior resonates with you, or it doesn't. And when it resonates with you it starts to bother you. And if it doesn't resonate with you, you wave and you say have a good day and you drive off. Does that make sense? Are there other questions?

Participant 2: *For example, you were talking about marriage, and this... is there any possibility to make it OK?*

What We would say is that everything is about frequency of vibration. So, if you are at frequency 352 and when you come and meet your partner they are within that range of resonance, so let's say between 340-360. You are in a similar range of resonance, and you continue along together, and then something happens in your life, for example, you have a child, and the amount of love that you feel you're your child shifts you into a different vibration, where you are at 500. But the husband is still a 352. And you start to split in your resonance with each other, there comes a distance. So, in that distance, there is the possibility, if you believe that the other will match you, perhaps they also go through a transmutation, and they come and match you. Perhaps you decide to go back down to their frequency, or perhaps you move beyond that to 700. There may come a point where you will no longer be in each other's experience. Relationships are based on resonance, and when there is no longer an energetic resonance, they are no longer your mirror.

You assume that they are fixed in stone. All that is fixed is that this world is a mirror to you. But it is dynamic, and the assumption that you will have the same mirror reflection constantly is an assumption. You might want the same mirror, and so therefore in wanting the same mirror, there is the possibility of enabling. So, if you are rising in vibratory spectrum, then through your own shift in vibration, they automatically shift. Not by you nagging them, go to this workshop. But that they experience your vibration, witnessing the Divinity within you, and that transmutes them automatically. But you can't say 'I'm so amazing, I am so enlightened and my husband sucks'. And assume that that's going to transmute their vibration. They transmute through you being Divine, through you seeing them through Our eyes and speaking to them with Our words and hearing them with Our ears. And behaving with them through Our inspiration. And it's not only a partner, it's that all of humanity can transmute when you allow Us to see through you, flow through you and speak through you.

That is how transmutation occurs. It is not by saying 'You need to shapen up because I'm enlightened and you who is separate from me, is not'. Because they're not separate from you, they are an extension of you. It is like you cannot see your cheek, but you can see your hand. They are like your hand. Does that make sense? They are merely the extension showing you what is it about you, you need to understand. So, do you need to stay in a marriage for life? Of course, if there is resonance you can, if there isn't resonance, why would you? Does that make sense? And it is not about suppressing things, as we mentioned, fear, anger, and frustration, they are all frequencies of emotion highlighting something to you. So, in the release of the fear, and in the release of the frustration, and in the release of the anger, not the suppression of it, but the processing and the transmutation of it - you reach a point where there is still no resonance, then there is no need to persist. Does that make sense?

Does the rain fall on the same flower and say, 'I am only going to drop on that flower?', or the sun decides this is the piece of land I am going to light up, the rest of it is off-limits?'. We would say that there is the assumption that there is an ownership of some sort in a partnership. But that is just demonstrative of the complete lack of understanding of why two people come together. And love is the holding of space for Divine flow, and if in a relationship Divine does not flow through both of you, there is no need to continue in that relationship, in the way that it is. So, if you're in a relationship where you are caged, if someone tells your partner, 'I saw your partner talking to someone' and then you come home and you get lectured for it. Is that the allowance of Divine flow? And We would say 'What is it in your belief system that makes you think that you shouldn't be A: talking to another person or B: that the partner has the right to dictate to you how you should behave?'. You choose to be the prisoner to others when you are free. And so, in love, love is just merely holding of space for others, because love is a frequency that interpermeates everything.

And when that frequency is blocked and is not allowed to flow. It's not love. It's rooted in low frequencies in the solar plexus and down, so it's rooted in fears, jealousy, anger, non-acceptance, judgment, shame, and guilt. They are not love. And when one loves themselves enough, then they decide that they no longer want to be caged. They decide and know that they are worthy to speak to whoever they want to. Because in their speaking to another perhaps an aspect of their Divinity can shine, so why would they deprive themselves of that? Why would they deprive the world of that? Because someone has fear? It is their fear. Their own fear that if they shine too brightly what might happen? And so, the starting point is always about self-love. When you are full, the world around you reflects back this fullness.

The decision is not about whether or not to stay in the marriage. The first question is, 'Is this relationship reflective of unconditional love for myself, and therefore as a result for everything else, or not?'. And it's not about the partner, it's about you. So, you ask yourself, 'If I love myself truly, unconditionally what would I do differently?'. And that changes for different people. One person would say 'If I love myself unconditionally, I wouldn't allow anyone to see my skin'. And someone else's is 'If I love myself unconditionally, I'll feel very safe to walk around naked'. Is one better than the other? You know they're both valid perspectives. So, what is true for you may not be true for society. What is true for you may not be true for the partner. What is true for you may not be true for others, but what is true for you is true for you. And that is what you're working with. And then eventually you shift into all of these beliefs, to the point where you understand that if a belief is this finite, then it's not serving my soul. And if it's demonstrative of that which is infinite then it is aligned with my soul.

So, what you wear is finite because it can change every day. So, it has nothing to do with the soul. Makes sense? It's not about the clothing. It's about the freedom. And the soul is free. So, control in any aspect is finite. OK? And so, as We were saying, that in the surrender and the trust of Divine's perfect magnificent orchestration for you, there is no need to limit yourself as to what should be. By deciding that you in your mind know better from your limited perspective when there is an omniscient perspective that knows the future, knows the past, knows the present, knows everything that is within you, everything that is creating disalignment, everything that enhances alignment, and has the omnipotent power to reorchestrate the entire universe just perfectly for you. But yet there is this resistance to allow that to happen because of the conditioning that 'I know better'. So, We're going to do an exercise, if you're ready.

B. Exercise 3: Gratitude for Creation & Surrender

The purpose of this exercise is to help remind you to be grateful for creation, of how Divine orchestrates the most magnificent systems and unfolding, and to allow you to experience the vibration of surrender.

There is a pillar of white luminescent light coming down from the sky, it is entering through the top of your head.

There is a pillar of white luminescent light coming down from the sky entering through the top of your head and lighting up your body. And as it reaches the heart level, it starts to radiate out of the heart forming a pyramid of white light around you.

There is a pillar of white luminescent light coming down from the sky, it is entering through the top of your head lighting up your body and radiating out the heart, forming a pyramid of white light around you.

And you call on Divine to make itself known to you. And you feel the shift in vibration.

There is a pillar of white luminescent light coming down from the sky and it is filling this room, it lights you up and radiates out through your heart forming a pyramid of light.

There's a pillar of white luminescent light coming down from the sky and it is filling this room, it lights you up and radiates out of the heart forming a pyramid of light around the building.

And the crown starts to expand even further so that more of this light gushes through you.

And the heart expands further. So that this river of light flows through and out of your heart in its full intensity, it is so bright.

And you know with all certainty this is Divine light that is gushing through you and out of you and surrounding you.

And you're going to focus on the heart. As you zoom into the heart you see yourself sitting in a comfortable space.

And you observe yourself or see how comfortable you are. And you're grateful.

And you look at the body that you are within. And you're grateful for it bringing you this far.

And you zoom out further. And you see the ground. And you're grateful for the ground. And all of the minerals and elements it provides.

And from the ground you see trees rising. And flowers blooming and you're grateful for their cleansing.

You're grateful for their witnessing. The trees are growing and rising around you. And you feel how they take care of you. How they love you and how you love them.

And you feel how the ground a solid beneath you. Firm and nurturing and you are grateful for this earth.

And as you zoom out further you see the animals and you're grateful for their company, for their teachings, for their properties, their vibrations, the signs that they give, the lessons that you can learn from. You are grateful for these animals. And their diversity.

And you zoom out further and you see the sea. And you are grateful for the sea that swallows all of your pain and disintegrates it. It absorbs all suffering and removes it from consciousness.

And you expand out further and you are grateful for the wind. The reminder to you, that We love you. And whenever you feel a breeze, you know it Us whispering, telling you that you're loved.

And you zoom out, pass the atmosphere, into space. And you look down on the earth. And notice that you can carry this earth in your hands. It is yours.

And that when you feel sadness, this entire earth feels your sadness. When you feel joy, the entire earth feels your joy.

And you set an intention for this earth. That despair is replaced with hope. And fear is replaced with love. And judgment is replaced with acceptance. And disconnection is replaced with Oneness.

And you see how this earth in your hands is transmuting. And listening to your loving intention. You observe how the world is changing, just with your intention, from the frequency of gratitude.

And then you zoom out past the universe that you observe the universe. And look down on it. And you see stars and planets and moons. All move in their measured portion, which appears to be physical matter and the movement of the frequency of vibration.

And the stars and the moons and the planets move at varying frequencies of vibration but each in their pattern and rhythm. And those in a similar frequency fall within a system. And the other systems have other frequencies.

When you look at the whole universe, from the space of love, infusing it with love, transmuting any systems of lower frequency than love, to that of love.

And you watch how they start to change their patterns of movement.

And then you ask Us: 'What does surrender mean? what does it mean to surrender to the Divine Will?'.

And when you're ready, you come back to your body, fully present in this time and space.

C. Poem: Shifting into Gratitude

'On your heads, We place a crown.
It is not that We look down,
It is that We draw you to expansion
To not limit you with ration
But enter into a splendor
So that you can remember
From where it is you came.
It is not about your fame,
It is that you are a part of Us.
So why is it, then, that you do not trust
That Our Will is always kind,
Kinder than the logical mind?

And We have offered you mountains and seas
And even with that, you are not pleased

And so, We show you the stars in the night
But then from the night, you take fright.
And so, the sun rises in the morn
And in the dread of your day, We are torn.
Torn by the reasons why you cannot see
Because those reasons keep you from being free –
From the limitations that you construct;
The flow of Our love, you obstruct.
And then you say that We have forsaken you,
Unaware of what it is you do.

It is through you that We can shine,
And through you, Our music can chime.

All We request is your grace
To shift to gratitude as the human race,
And then all Our yearnings can unfold
And blissful stories can be told
In the unraveling of a Divine earth.
It is through you that We take birth.

Thank you.'

5. OPENING YOURSELF TO RECEIVE

A. Giving & Collective Benefit

So, we're going to talk about the second key ingredient for manifestation. So, the first is that of gratitude or the vibration of gratitude or higher than that. So, any vibratory spectrum of Divinity from the heart, the throat, the Ajna, or the crown that enables manifestation. And the second ingredient is opening up, to be able to receive. And how does one open up to be able to receive? They offer themself to others. So, in the same way, when you do your channeling process, you receive through the crown, and you release through the heart. Energy is continuous flow and if it is blocked from flowing either at the offering or the entering point, there will be no possibility for manifestation according to your yearning.

And so if you were to imagine the cycle of this flow of energy. The components are in that you receive it, but you also offer. And so, that which you would like to receive, you offer the same spectrum. So, if you want to be accepted, you yourself accept. Accept yourself and accept others. If you want to be loved, then you love yourself. And you love others. And again, love is the offering of space for Divinity to shine. So, you assume that love only comes for example in a romantic relationship that you have, love is in every interaction, every experience that you have. And so, the compounding of this vibration enables the flow of it, or the attraction of this vibration to you, the reflection of this vibration to you, and the more that you offer it, the more

THE KEYS TO MANIFESTATION

it compounds and the more it flows back. The more loving, the more you experience that love.

Because in the remembrance that you are not separate from that which is in the world around you, by you being that what you see outside of you also is. If you want health. What is health rooted in? Alignment of the soul. So, the enablement of the alignment of your soul or the assistance of others in their alignment of their soul. Not by instructing them, but by loving them, the same way by loving yourself. Health is a natural byproduct of alignment. And the natural byproduct of disalignment is disease.

You want wealth? You offer wealth. Because whatever you give is compounded in its returning back to you as a frequency of vibration. It is for example, you are at a lake, and you throw in a stone, the stone drops in, but then the ripples expand and compound outwards. So, one would say 'But if I am short of money I can't afford to give', as an example. But you can give in many ways. So, you give what you feel that you can. You can offer your skill, to aid someone so that they don't have to pay for something. Or you give what you already have that you don't need. Or you give what you want because in holding on to what you have, you stop the flow. And then the offering of all you have, the return flow is abundant and infinite beyond your comprehension.

We will give a simple example, of how this compounded influence can occur. You live in a neighborhood. And your neighbor, for example, has just given birth and doesn't have the time to cook. And yet you are worried about having enough resources for food. But you cook for your neighbor, out of love. Because they're your neighbor, and you love them, and you want to ease their burden. From a genuine intention of love. Not only intention of I scratch your back you scratch my back. But from a loving vibration. Or it can even be that I remember when I gave birth my neighbor was so kind and helped me and so I, in that gratitude, I offered the same. So you cook for your neighbor. And then what happens?

The neighbor finds out that you're in need. And they say when I was in need you were there to help me. But maybe, as the neighbor, they were not in a position to help you. So, they're at a dinner party somewhere else and they say to their friend: 'Actually the thing that got me through my delivery was that my neighbor used to cook for me.' And then someone at that dinner says, 'Oh, who was that?', and they name you. And the next thing you know you get a call, and that person says, 'Would you like a job? Because I understand that from your neighbor that you have the skills that we require'. And it just comes back full circle. Did you plan it? No. We planned it. It doesn't need to be through your control, nor you deciding on how you're going to get a job. How is money going to come to you? When you do things from the heart with a genuine high vibratory frequency, We would say that it is near impossible that it will not come back compounded. And it will come back again in the area where you are in need.

Because We know what your needs are, and We know what your earnings are. We know what your insecurities are, and your fears. So, when you act from the space of love, it is impossible for you not to receive Divine love back. And as you love in finite measure, We love in infinite measure. Does that make sense? And then one would say, OK, so if I feed my neighbor should I tell everyone that I did it just to make sure that everyone knows that I helped her, and then

THE KEYS TO MANIFESTATION

someone will give me a job? It's not necessary and by doing that perhaps it dilutes the intention.

So, is it to say through generosity you should never speak of it? Depends on the vibration with which you give it, is of love, and if you speak of it, it is from ego. So, the ball that is projected drops. Whereas you give from love, but then from Oneness, there is the intention for this to become a norm, or you for example, form a charity, where there's the possibility that mothers who give birth are then able to be fed by their neighbors, as an example. And you use your story as an example. Is that dropping it to ego? Or is that moving it to a higher vibration? So that more of the community can experience the same.

So, there is no rule. People like to make rules. Like 'You give but you don't talk about it'. Depends on why you want to talk about it. What are you doing to the vibration of that action? because the action's intention was in a vibration. If you're going to elevate that vibration, then elevate it. But We would suggest don't take further action to reduce the vibration. Does that make sense? People like to invest in the stock market. Maybe they get a 7% return, or they put their money in the bank on fixed deposit, so they get their 1.25% return, but it's safe there, they are not going to lose it. It's very safe for them. And so, they're in fear, fear of the future. Fear of what is to come, that they cannot trust that they will be taken care of. But do you need to hoard it?

Because although you hoard it and invest it, in the stock market or the bank, perhaps there will be a stock market crash. Perhaps the bank will go bust. Is that within your control? And then you could say 'It's because there was a lousy CEO at the bank', that's why it went bust. And We would say it's also beyond his control or her control. It is the reflection of collective consciousness, and the way in which society or economics exists is from a space of fear, greed, and separation. Where competition is the intention, to be the winner, as opposed to seeing that as a species, as beings in this realm, together there is the possibility through collaboration for further enhancement and expansion. And if We were to say, in the way that businesses are progressing, as an example, the businesses that use collaboration as the foundations of their platform, are the ones that thrive and grow. Because now is the time for collaboration.

Amazon doesn't offer its own products. They collaborate with thousands of suppliers and networks. And although there is still the notion of competition that they should be the largest retailer, there will come a point, where competition will cease to exist, and collaboration will be what is dominant. Because as a collective consciousness, there is a shifting to action driven from the heart, as opposed to action driven from the ego. Where in the ego there is this individualistic approach that one is better than the other, or identity, and at the heart there is a community. You are connected with others. And so, through this connection, is how flow compounds. And so, the flow compounds in business or it compounds as an individual by connecting and offering a possibility, offering of Divine vibration. This is what opens the door.

With no offering, the door stays locked and then there is the limit of how much you can fill yourself with. As We mentioned earlier this morning, perhaps the 5000-pound lottery ticket seems OK. The 160 million seems impossible, because you have this limit set, whereas if the door is open and the flow just gushes through, and you're just part of the ocean, then there's no limit. So, it is not only from the individualized perspective but from the collective consciousness perspective, it is the same. And in the way that functions, there is the functionality of community, societies, and economies or politics, it is the same way you function as an individual. The communal is reflective of communal consciousness. Makes sense?

So, if We were to say, that as an individual your goal is to shine in magnificent light. Wouldn't it also be as a collective that the goal would be to shine in magnificent light? So, how can it be that you shine, and another doesn't? And organizations, communities, societies - they are all just merely collections of people who are either shining or dimmed. So as an individual, in order for the opening of abundance to be received, there is the offering and the gratitude in the launch of intent. The same way for organizations, or communities, or families, or countries... it is the same.

So, you can watch the unfolding of how things will progress, and communities where there is this separation will no longer be able to thrive as the earth transmutes. Organizations focused on separation will not survive. And in the same way, individuals focused on separation will feel uncomfortable and not thrive. It is not because they are being punished, it is because they are in disalignment. And that first perhaps there is a nudge, and then there is a shake, and no matter how deaf one chooses to be to the inner guidance, there will come a point where it can no longer be ignored, because there is a Universal plan for the transmutation of consciousness.

B.   Q&A Section

Does anyone have any questions?

Participant 1: *What is greed?*

It is the shadow opposite of gratitude. So, there is always a tipping point for any frequency of vibration. In that from one aspect, greed is the non-trust of Divine abundance and gratitude can be the absolute trust of Divine abundance. So, in greed, there is the notion that there is lack or scarcity, 'I must have more', for whatever reason. And the root of it can be many. But it is rooted in the lack of trust in the Divine. And it starts the separation. So as an individual or a community, the more movement into the spectrum of greed, away from that of gratitude... so if you imagine a ruler and then the center is the balance or the tipping point and, in the spectrum, there is gratitude, increasing in intensity and in the spectrum, there is greed, increasing in its intensity.

The tipping point in the center is neutral. But when you move along the spectrum of greed you will fall further into disconnection, and when you move along the spectrum of gratitude you fall further in connection. And so, in gratitude and connection, your experience becomes more and more blissful. The more you move along the spectrum, the more magnificent and miraculous the experience. And in greed, and the more disconnection, the more suffering, discontent, and discomfort. Because you are moving further into disconnection, so it can be on an individual level or a collective consciousness level.

Participant 1: *Can I follow it up with another question?*

Yes.

Participant 1: *If one would have 50$ in the pocket. And they see something they want for 50$, and there's the option of using this 50$ to help someone. At that point there is sometimes a dilemma, am I being greedy in buying that thing that I want? I know I can take either decision, but there's the question, am I being greedy by not sharing?*

What We would say is that is a misuse of term or terminology. So, in the dilemma, there is the decision that it's either one or the other. Because in the logical perspective, fifty dollars is only fifty dollars. And what We would say is that before deciding anything, you need to ask yourself 'What is that thing going to give me? Why do I need it? Why do I want it?', for example. And then you also look at the one who needs something, and you see 'What is the vibration I feel?'. If you're like, 'ah my fifty bucks.' And then you're grumpy all day, what was the point of that? Because you think you're bargaining with God? 'I'm doing what you told me, and I hate every minute of it but I'm going to do it. But I hate it. And I wanted that pair of shoes which were sparkly and perfect but I'm doing what you told me and I'm giving it to the poor guy, but I want the shoes', how is that beneficial to you?

Participant 1: *It's not, it doesn't sound that morbid. But there is a bit of guilt.*

What We would say is that in the offering of something to another. It is not you who's doing anything. We are doing it and using you as the mailbox. So, when the offering... if someone comes to you to ask for something or you see someone suffering and you feel inclined to help them, be thankful you have been chosen as the vehicle to deliver. Because out of the seven billion other vehicles that are possible, you have been given this opportunity. And you are given that opportunity because you are resonating in that vibration.

Participant 2: *Can I ask another question?*

Yes.

Participant 2: *Sometimes there are beggars that you feel not positive to give anything, and to some, you really feel like giving most of the things that you have in your hand. I have been to places where there are a lot of beggars and they are very aggressive and they are very dangerous, they threaten you, curse you. I don't feel like giving them, is it something in me? Should I give them? And how to distinguish do you give them or not?*

So, as We had said, anything external of you is a reflection of your internal. They are an extension of you, and if they make you feel uncomfortable, you need to address 'What is this discomfort within?'. Do you have to give them something when you feel uncomfortable? Of course not. Because it will make you feel even more uncomfortable. So, walk away and address what is it that bothered you about that. Is it that you felt unsafe, and why do you feel unsafe? Are you not taken care of? Are you not protected? When you feel completely safe and protected, you won't see beggars like that anyway. But there is an underlying insecure feeling, an underlying lack of trust, which brings scenarios to you to highlight to you that yes there is something in me where I don't feel safe. I don't feel secure. And that is what is to be released. The beggar to you is just the puppet responding to the script of your command (the script of your movie).

And so, when you see someone, the ones that you say you feel like giving them everything, that is also the response to your script. Does that make sense? Does the script need to be the same every day? It fluctuates, some days you feel better than others. Some days you're more aligned than others. Is it to say because you saw a beggar that made you feel unsafe ten years ago, that it's going to keep repeating if you've already released that sense of insecurity? No, but maybe the next time you see the beggar, from ten years ago and you see his face and for some reason you smile, and you say come here and you give them a hug, 'How are you doing?', for example.

It is just a reflection of you. What is it that you need to deal with? And then you could say 'I see a beggar who is a drug addict or an alcoholic'. It is not about the judgment, because in actuality if you judge them to say, 'I'm not going to give them money because they're going to be drinking', for example. You're not judging them, you're judging yourself. They are merely an extension of you. So you see them, and you judge them, and perhaps you say, 'They're not worthy of love', because you believe you're not worthy of love. Because the one who believes they are worthy of love and knows that they are loved, doesn't choose who to share that love with. A flower smells sweet for whoever wishes to smell it. But doesn't decide, whether or not you're worthy of taking a sniff. Because it is aligned and has no barriers or layers, and so it blooms in its magnificence.

So, We would say, in the resistance of offering, it is always highlighting something to you. So that you can reach the space where you are grateful that you can be a vehicle to help someone else. You're grateful for what you have. Or you're grateful to just be the tool. And does it mean that once you have reached a certain point you will never drift back? Of course there will be fluctuations in your day to day.

Participant 3: *Can I ask a question?*

Yes.

Participant 3: *Speaking about fear, I don't understand from where we get fear from. I mean this fear of anything, like for example I would like to say about myself. I used to think that I feared something specific, of failure, not being successful. But with time I feel I have a fear of a lot of things. Now I fear heights, I fear excitement, extreme excitement, I fear many things. I feel that it's just multiplying. And it's just growing rapidly. And then you want to be in this bubble, kind of you don't want to have many experiences because you just don't want to expose your emotions to that feeling of anxiety and fear.*

So, fear is the root of separation. It is the frequency that creates duality. So, in measured portion it enables experience, but in compounded portion, it prevents experience as you have described. And so, if there is the slipping into this, fear, or disconnection, then there is the limitation of what can be possible. And We would say what is the root of this fear? it lies in the root chakra. And it is about trusting in Divine Orchestration. And so, you can do your resolution on when it was that you first started to lose trust and let it go. It's not to say that you should be fearless, but when it takes over, as you mentioned, it limits possibility. And if anything, all of these fears are merely reflections to you highlighting you don't need to be afraid, you can trust Us.

For example, you have your child. And your child wants to go play. And so, you say, OK, make sure that you are supervised by an adult. And make sure that you dress appropriately. Put the proper clothes on, make sure that you have your coat, it might be cold. And you fuss over the child and then you keep on saying, are you sure you did this? Are you sure you did this? Check the shoes, check the socks. Making sure everything is OK. And then they want to go ice skating and you think yes you definitely need warm clothes. So, you bundle them up even more. The scarf comes out, the mittens come out, the hat comes out, extra jacket. And they go to the ice-skating rink and before they get on the ice, you say, 'No, no, put the knee pads on, and the helmet'. And they are ice skating, and you think OK they're safe my friend is looking after them everything is OK. And then you get a call from your friend, that your child ate popcorn and choked on it. Doesn't matter how much you try to protect them. If something is in the path to occur, it will happen, and if something is not in the path to occur, it won't happen. So, they choked on it, someone does the Heimlich Maneuver, out comes the popcorn, everything's fine. So next time you go to the ice-skating rink, no popcorn. And then they might almost get burned by a coffee. There are infinite things that can go wrong.

Participant 3: *That's where fear sets in.*

Exactly, so you just need to trust that what is meant to be, will be. They are held in Our embrace.

Participant 4: *So, whatever is meant to happen, will happen.*

Yes.

Participant 4: *There is no need for fear?*

There is no need for fear.

Participant 4: *Let go of control.*

You cannot control, the unfolding of experience, for the child to witness their light. Because you might try to dim it. But eventually, they have their own journey, and there will be resistance in that they choose to express it regardless. Allow them to shine. Allow yourself to shine and allow everyone in your life to shine. So that everything can be in

THE KEYS TO MANIFESTATION

magnificence and trust that you are all looked after, so that this light can shine. Because We also have Our agenda that we want to shine. And we will ensure that it will because that is the Divine plan. So, in that plan, you can struggle, and fuss about the coats, the knee pads, and the extra socks. Or you can hug your child before they go and say, have a fabulous time, have fun. It's up to you. Control is an illusion. Because anything that is in the shadow of truth is merely an illusion, or delusion. So, truth is freedom. Controlling is a limitation. It is something that is finite. And in its property of being finite, it cannot cover everything. And there will be the examples of what was missed, so that there was the recognition, that not everything can be covered. And when there is the acknowledgment that, 'Yes I can't control everything, I let go and I surrender to God.' Then plop! No need to suffer anymore. Okay?

Participant 2: *Can you tell us more please, about possibilities and how to be able to hear their guidance, and how to take an action in which you stay in connection, and when to let go of something?*

So, the question is about the magnificent possibility and how to act on it or recognize what it is. So, in the recognition of what it is, what We would say is, that whatever feels blissful is a magnificent possibility, and whatever doesn't feel blissful, is not. Simple. Because high vibrational emotions, demonstrate alignment, and low vibratory emotions demonstrate disalignment. They are merely the barometer of check, it's like your checklist, 'I feel good, yes', 'I don't feel good, no'. Very simple. And then how to take action based on it? Allow it's unfolding. Listen to that inner voice. Channel about it. And We don't mean channel about it on the first of January and then the next time you ask about it is the following year. It should be part of your continuous connection. Because in every moment there are infinite possibilities. And there is the magnificent one within the infinite. Every moment you take one step, infinite possibilities open, and one is lit up as the magnificent one, and then you take another step, again infinite possibilities open up. Right? So, it's to be in a constant state of listening, allowance of this flow, the allowance of Us to speak through you, for you to hear with Our ears, to see with Our eyes, to act with Our guidance.

And is it that your magnificent possibility is always going to look from the picture perspective as the perfect one? In actuality, it can be on presentation the worst thing that could have possibly happened to you. You might lose a child. But that doesn't mean it's not your magnificent possibility. It is the scenario in which you will reach absolute alignment with your soul. And because you don't have full data in your logic, you assume something is terrible. But from an omniscient perspective, it is something that is magnificent for the experience of Divinity. And sometimes, as We mentioned, there is the nudging and the whisper, and the pushing. And there is continuous ignorance... ignoring of the signs until the sign needs to be strong enough for you to listen.

Are We the one who is torturing you or depriving you? You've been depriving yourself all along. So, for example, someone does poorly in their high school exams. And everyone on the external says, 'It's a disaster, they're going to be a loser. Now what? They won't be able to get into any university, they're doomed!'. Are they? What do they believe will happen? They are magnificent beings of light. And there are infinite ways for them to express that light. Infinite paths. But as parents you say, 'No, engineering, medicine, psychology', whatever... you have your checklist, this is good, the rest is not so good. But if as a species every single being is uniquely diverse not only in their spectrum of vibration but in the dynamic form of the spectrum of vibration, therefore every instant is diverse. How can it be that everyone needs to be an engineer? And most certainly when things occur that you feel are completely out of your control or completely out of thought reference, then they are most certainly part of the magnificent unfolding. OK?

Participant 4: *If things are going out of control, it is the part of magnificent possibility?*

It depends, what is the software that you replay? If every day you say everything is a disaster everything will be a disaster until you decide it's not a disaster because it isn't a disaster. It's the window with which you choose to view things.

Participant 4: *There was one statement that they (channel) mentioned one day: that I deserve the best. And since that sentence there was a massive shift in my life for the better. It seems to people that I am in misery, but I am not in misery. I am being elevated towards a better life. Because of one positive statement, sometimes I say to myself.*

We would say what anyone else thinks is irrelevant, it's what you think that is relevant and it is what you think that is reflected back to you.

Participant 4: *I felt the Divine love, I felt that I am taken care of. I feel that I need to trust the Divine in all the steps in my life.*

Good.

Thank you.

C. Exercise 4: Giving & Receiving

This is an exercise to do in channel and make notes:

1. What are the things that you want to experience in your life?
2. Channel where they sit in the body, what is driving these wants? Ego? Fear? Divine?
3. Write down the ones that are below the heart chakra level and burn the list.
4. Reflect on the ways you give in your life. What are the things you feel comfortable giving? Where do you feel uncomfortable giving? Channel about why this is so.
5. Channel about how to make giving a more natural flow in your life, and the ways you can open up to give in particular the areas where you hold back.

THE KEYS TO MANIFESTATION

D. Exercise 5: Manifestation of a Vibration

This exercise is about pulling in energies or vibrations from the astral realm, into physicality.

OK so if you just relax, we're going to do the final exercise.

Focus on the center of your chest, and in the center of the chest, you're going to see a seed of golden light.

The seed of golden light is the light of Divine, of Divine love, and the seed is going to start to spin and rotate faster and faster until it forms a ball of golden light in the center of the chest.

And this ball of light is going to keep expanding with every inhalation and exhalation of golden light and is expanding and becoming brighter and brighter, expanding beyond your body.

And this golden light of love, you feel this light of love expanding further and further, filling the space where you are.

Let this light of Divine love that's radiating out, and you're going to call on Divine love to be known to you. You say, 'I call on Divine love to be known to me'. Allow it to amplify you say 'Amplify, become brighter, and intensify'.

This light of love is so bright it is almost solid. Even though it expands further, the further it expands, the brighter it becomes.

Then you're just going to put your hands on the chest and move into this vibration of gratitude, starting with the gratitude for this body, your vessel that you are, that you have.

Grateful for the body that enables you to live, to see, and to love.

Just focus on this gratitude for this possibility to love. To love the self and to love others. To love those close to you and those who you don't even know. To love this earth and all its creatures.

Focus on this gratitude. You are able to love.

And then you're going to focus on your mind and be grateful for your mind. This mind that has all of these thoughts, this mind that is able to dream, imagine and hope. This mind that is able to witness, understand and comprehend. Just feel gratitude for your mind.

And now, be grateful for the air. Grateful for the air that you're able to breathe. The light around you. The things that you are able to feel and experience.

The journeys you have been on in your life, and the places you've been to, and the people you have been able to meet. Just focus on gratitude for this life even if there are ups and downs. So much you have been able to live, to experience, to witness.

And in this space of gratitude, you're just going to express what it is that you want, as a vibration, not as a thing. So, this vibration perhaps of freedom, this vibration of vitality, vibration of love, abundance, connection, joy.

You focus on these vibrations that you want to pull into your life. And you accept that you don't need to decide how it comes in, or when it comes in, or through who it comes in, but you just, in this activated heart, connect to the astral dimension, expressing 'I call on joy', for example, 'And draw it to my life'.

And then you just feel this vibration of joy filling your body and you express 'I am so grateful for this joy', and then you can for example call in the next vibration. 'I call on love into my life or connection or belonging'.

Whatever it is that you want, call on that vibration and draw it into your life. As you call it from the astral into your life and you say, 'I draw on this vibration of...', you can fill the blank and feel this vibration in your body that you have called for, whatever it is: the freedom, the connectivity, the abundance, bliss, the love...

Just feel your body expanding in this vibration or vibrations and express the gratitude that you are grateful to be able to feel this.

You draw it to your life and you say 'I call on whatever it is', for example security, or trust, or your home, whatever it is that you are yearning for - feel it as a vibration. It isn't a thing. It is the feeling - call on this vibration and you say, 'I draw you in from the astral into my life' and feel this vibration fill your physical body, express gratitude, 'Thank you for this', whatever it is that you called on. 'I'm grateful'.

And if there are other vibrations you want to call on, you call on them. You say 'I draw this vibration into my life from the astral. I am calling this vibration of ....'. You fill the blank and you feel it, you see the energy flowing to you from the astral plane, drawing it into your physical life, as it fills your body.

You don't need to imagine it in your house or in your life, or you're at some place. You draw this vibration into your physical body, as your physical body is part of this physical dimension.

Feel this vibration in your body and express gratitude that it is manifested in your physicality. It has merged in your physicality.

You can say 'I am grateful for this merging of energy in my physicality'. Focus on the gratitude as it has merged into your physical experience.

And then you say 'I allow this vibration to integrate into my physicality with no expectation or attachment of the shape it must take. I surrender this manifestation to Divine's orchestration, which will be beyond what my mind can dream of'.

Express gratitude for this Divine orchestration.

When you are ready, you come back to your body fully present in this time and space, with all of your personality and consciousness fully present in this time and space.

6. CONCLUSION

In summary, the formula for abundance and manifestation is GIVING + GRATITUDE.

- *Gratitude: Maintain a vibration of the heart chakra or higher.*
- *Giving: Open the room to flow. Give what you want to receive, and it will be compounded back to you multifold more. But giving should be from the heart chakra vibration or higher.*

Furthermore, there is no need to limit the abundance based on your beliefs and frame of reference. Allow Divine's orchestration of flow to manifest a more beautiful offering than your mind could ever have thought of. Let your fears, insecurities, mind, and ego step out of the way of Divine's love. As Divine is always loving you.

With love,

From all of us at Dira

ABOUT THE AUTHOR

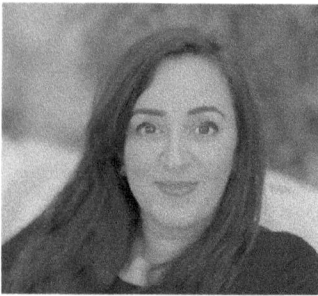

Lubna Kharusi is the Founder of Dira and is one of the clearest channelers of Divine Source on the earth today and teaches people how to also become channels of Source.

She was born in the Sultanate of Oman. She is a Chartered Accountant, a trained hypnotherapist, and her Master's thesis was on 'Happiness'. She was the Chief Financial Officer of a multi-billion-dollar government company in Oman. As an unfolding of her spiritual journey, she left her successful career and founded Dira International. Dira's vision is the transmutation of vibration of the world and cosmos, to enable the shift of collective consciousness from separation to Oneness, by using The Dira Method.

The Dira Method was channeled by Lubna, and she has channeled thousands of sessions relating to different forms of transmutation, explanations, and guidance for humanity that enable a shift in the participants, their lives, community, and eventually the world.

In addition, she holds channeled retreats and workshops on various subjects for varying purposes. She is the author of 10 books including 'For Humanity'.

In collaboration with IONS, Lubna and Dira channelers were studied and The Dira Method is referenced in the book 'The Science of Channeling' by the world's leading scientific expert on channeling, Helane Wahbeh, as a method for anyone to learn how to channel.

In 2019, in honour and recognition of her work with Dira, she was honoured and appointed by the late Sultan Qaboos bin Said Al Said of Oman to the State Council: The Upper House of Oman's Parliament.

Books by Lubna Kharusi

1. For Humanity, Volume 1
2. I Love you More Than…
3. Fly my Little Butterfly
4. Made of Love
5. I am Perfect
6. Happiness in the Quran
7. Oman: The Journey of Light
8. Dira Basic Channeling – Accessing Divine Consciousness
9. Dira Advanced Channeling – How to Use Channeling to Change Your Life
10. Activate Your Abundance - The Keys to Manifestation

www.ingramcontent.com/pod-product-compliance
Lightning Source LLC
LaVergne TN
LVHW010318070426
835508LV00033B/3497